PRESIDENTS

CHESTER A. ARTHUR

A MyReportLinks.com Book

Jeff C. Young

MyReportLinks.com Books

an imprint of

Enslow Publishers, Inc. E

Box 398, 40 Industrial Road
Berkeley Heights, NJ 07922
USA

To my grandparents, Leeland Nelson Hanna and Melba Perkins Hanna

MyReportLinks.com Books, an imprint of Enslow Publishers, Inc. MyReportLinks is a trademark of Enslow Publishers, Inc.

Library of Congress Cataloging-in-Publication Data

Young, Jeff C., 1948–
      Chester A. Arthur / Jeff C. Young.
         p. cm. — (Presidents)
      Summary: A biography of the twenty-first president of the United States, focusing on his personal life, education, and political career. Includes Internet links to Web sites, source documents, and photographs related to Chester Arthur.
      Includes bibliographical references and index.
      ISBN 0-7660-5077-7
      1. Arthur, Chester Alan, 1829–1886—Juvenile literature. 2. Presidents—United States—Biography—Juvenile literature. [1. Arthur, Chester Alan, 1829–1886. 2. Presidents.] I. Title. II. Series.
E692.Y68 2002
973.8′4′092—dc21
[B]   2001008191

Printed in the United States of America

10 9 8 7 6 5 4 3 2 1

To Our Readers:
Through the purchase of this book, you and your library gain access to the Report Links that specifically back up this book.

The Publisher will provide access to the Report Links that back up this book and will keep these Report Links up to date on **www.myreportlinks.com** for three years from the book's first publication date.

We have done our best to make sure all Internet addresses in this book were active and appropriate when we went to press. However, the author and the Publisher have no control over, and assume no liability for, the material available on those Internet sites or on other Web sites they may link to.

The usage of the MyReportLinks.com Books Web site is subject to the terms and conditions stated on the Usage Policy Statement on **www.myreportlinks.com**.

In the future, a password may be required to access the Report Links that back up this book. The password is found on the bottom of page 4 of this book.

Any comments or suggestions can be sent by e-mail to comments@myreportlinks.com or to the address on the back cover.

Photo Credits: © Corel Corporation, pp. 1 (background), 3; Courtesy of © 2000, The New York Times Company, p. 35; Courtesy of America's Story from America's Library/Library of Congress, pp. 11, 13; Courtesy of American Memory/Library of Congress, p. 33; Courtesy of *Dictionary of American Portraits*, Dover Publications, Inc., © 1967, pp. 20, 22, 26, 31, 36, 41; Courtesy of HarpWeek, pp. 27, 32; Courtesy of historicvermont.org, p. 15; Courtesy of MyReportLinks.com Books, p. 4; Courtesy of Smithsonian National Museum of American History, pp. 37, 44; Courtesy of The White House Web site, p. 30; Courtesy of Thinkquest Library, pp. 23, 38; Courtesy of U.S. Capitol Collection, p. 17; Library of Congress, p. 25, 28; National Archives, p. 21; Vermont District of Historic Preservation, p. 1.

Cover Photo: © Corel Corporation; Vermont District of Historic Preservation

Contents

MyReportLinks.com Books
Great Books, Great Links, Great for Research!

MyReportLinks.com Books present the information you need to learn about your report subject. In addition, they show you where to go on the Internet for more information. The pre-evaluated Report Links that back up this book are kept up to date on **www.myreportlinks.com**. With the purchase of a MyReportLinks.com Books title, you and your library gain access to the Report Links that specifically back up that book. The Report Links save hours of research time and link to dozens—even hundreds—of Web sites, source documents, and photos related to your report topic.

Please see "To Our Readers" on the Copyright page for important information about this book, the MyReportLinks.com Books Web site, and the Report Links that back up this book.

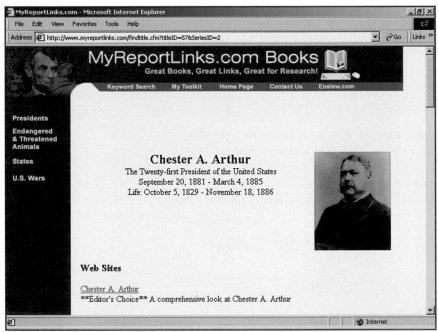

Access:

The Publisher will provide access to the Report Links that back up this book and will try to keep these Report Links up to date on our Web site for three years from the book's first publication date. Please enter **PAR1762** if asked for a password.

Report Links

The Internet sites described below can be accessed at
http://www.myreportlinks.com

*EDITOR'S CHOICE

▶**Chester A. Arthur**

Offering a plethora of resources relating to Chester A. Arthur, this site
contains an image gallery, quotes, links, and comprehensive articles
about his life and presidency.

Link to this Internet site from http://www.myreportlinks.com

*EDITOR'S CHOICE

▶**The American Presidency: Chester A. Arthur**

This biography of Chester A. Arthur discusses his life and presidency
with an emphasis on his relationship with Roscoe Conkling, his
battles with Congress, his reformation of civil service, and his
personal attributes.

Link to this Internet site from http://www.myreportlinks.com

*EDITOR'S CHOICE

▶**Chester Alan Arthur**

At this Web site you will find facts and figures about Chester A.
Arthur's life, career, and presidency. You also find many useful
links to Arthur's election results, Cabinet members, and other
Internet biographies.

Link to this Internet site from http://www.myreportlinks.com

*EDITOR'S CHOICE

▶**The American President: "Happenstance"**

At this PBS Web site you will learn about five vice presidents,
including Chester A. Arthur, who took over the office of the
presidency upon the death of a president. Here you will learn how
Arthur felt about moving into the role of president.

Link to this Internet site from http://www.myreportlinks.com

*EDITOR'S CHOICE

▶**American Presidents: Life Portraits**

This page is an outline of facts about Chester A. Arthur. Here you
will find "Did You Know?" trivia about Chester A. Arthur, a portrait
gallery, a letter written by Arthur, and a links to useful resources.

Link to this Internet site from http://www.myreportlinks.com

*EDITOR'S CHOICE

▶**Vermont State: Historic Sites: U.S. Presidents**

At this site you can explore the home of Chester A. Arthur in Fairfield,
Vermont. You will also find a biography about Chester A. Arthur and
an image of the church where Arthur's father often preached.

Link to this Internet site from http://www.myreportlinks.com

 The Internet sites described below can be accessed at
http://www.myreportlinks.com

▶ **America: The Great Melting Pot: Immigration**
This ThinkQuest Web site explores immigration in the United States. This section focuses on Chinese immigration beginning in the eighteenth century and how the Chinese Exclusion Act of 1882 affected Chinese immigrants.

Link to this Internet site from http://www.myreportlinks.com

▶ **Annual Messages to Congress on the State of the Union (1790–2002)**
At this Web site you will find Chester A. Arthur's messages to Congress. You will also find links to other United States presidents messages to Congress.

Link to this Internet site from http://www.myreportlinks.com

▶ **Archives of the West from 1877–1887**
At this PBS Web site you will find an extract from Chester A. Arthur's First Annual Address to Congress. This extract focuses on Indian Policy Reform.

Link to this Internet site from http://www.myreportlinks.com

▶ **Arthur, Chester Alan**
This general biography of President Chester A. Arthur covers his early life, legal career, political career, and presidency.

Link to this Internet site from http://www.myreportlinks.com

▶ **Biography of Chester Arthur**
The official White House biography of Chester A. Arthur highlights the important issues of his life and presidency.

Link to this Internet site from http://www.myreportlinks.com

▶ **Biography of Ellen Arthur**
The official White House Web site holds the biography of Ellen Arthur, Chester A. Arthur's wife who died in 1880, a few months before he was inaugurated.

Link to this Internet site from http://www.myreportlinks.com

Report Links

The Internet sites described below can be accessed at
http://www.myreportlinks.com

▶ **Charles J. Guiteau Shot President Garfield**
America's Story from America's Library, a Library of Congress Web
site provides a brief overview of James Garfield's assassination. After
the death of Garfield, Vice President Chester A. Arthur took the oath
of office.

Link to this Internet site from http://www.myreportlinks.com

▶ **Chester Alan Arthur**
At this Web site you will find a brief chronology of major events that
took place during Arthur's administration and a list of his Cabinet
members. You will also learn about his domestic and foreign policies.

Link to this Internet site from http://www.myreportlinks.com

▶ **Chester A. Arthur**
At this Web site you will find a biography of Chester A. Arthur. Here
you will learn about his life, marriage, vice presidency, and presidency.

Link to this Internet site from http://www.myreportlinks.com

▶ **Chester A. Arthur**
At this Web site you will find the biography of Chester A. Arthur. Here
you will learn about his life before, during, and after the presidency.

Link to this Internet site from http://www.myreportlinks.com

▶ **Chester A. Arthur**
This biography of Chester A. Arthur, in addition to discussing the
important events of his presidency, also gives information about his
parents, his wife, and other details.

Link to this Internet site from http://www.myreportlinks.com

▶ **Chester A. Arthur**
At the National Portrait Gallery you will find a painting by Ole Peter
Hansen Balling and a daguerreotype by Rufus Anson of Chester A.
Arthur. You will also find a brief description of the images and a brief
biography of Chester A. Arthur.

Link to this Internet site from http://www.myreportlinks.com

The Internet sites described below can be accessed at
http://www.myreportlinks.com

▶**Documents on Anti-Chinese Immigration Policy**
At this PBS Web site you can explore documents relating to the Anti-Chinese
Immigration Policy.

Link to this Internet site from http://www.myreportlinks.com

▶**Ellen Lewis Herndon Arthur**
At this Web site you will find the biography of Ellen Lewis Herndon Arthur.
Here you will learn about her life and marriage to Chester A. Arthur.

Link to this Internet site from http://www.myreportlinks.com

▶**Harpweek Elections 1884**
This time line explains important events that occurred during Chester A.
Arthur's presidency, including the Chinese Exclusion Act, the Pendleton Act,
the Mongrel Tariff bill, and Garfield's assassination.

Link to this Internet site from http://www.myreportlinks.com

▶**"I Do Solemnly Swear . . . "**
At this Web site you will find an image of Vice President Chester A. Arthur
taking the oath of presidency in his home on September 20, 1881.

Link to this Internet site from http://www.myreportlinks.com

▶**James Garfield: The Martyred President**
At this Web site you will find a comprehensive biography of James Garfield.
Here you will learn about his life, presidency, and assassination attempt that
occurred four months into his presidency.

Link to this Internet site from http://www.myreportlinks.com

▶**Mr. President: Chester A. Arthur**
At this Web site you will find a brief profile of Chester A. Arthur. Here you
learn about basic facts about Arthur and find a quote.

Link to this Internet site from http://www.myreportlinks.com

Report Links

 The Internet sites described below can be accessed at
http://www.myreportlinks.com

▶ News of Chester Arthur's Death
This article from the front page of the November 19, 1886, edition of
the the *New York Times*, is a resource that documents how the president
was viewed in his own time.

Link to this Internet site from http://www.myreportlinks.com

▶ Objects from the Presidency
At this site you will find information on all the presidents of the
United States, including Chester A. Arthur. Read a brief description
of the era he lived in and learn about the office of the presidency.

Link to this Internet site from http://www.myreportlinks.com

▶ On This Day: At Liberty's Door
At this Web site you will learn about the assassination of
President James Garfield and Chester A. Arthur's succession
to president.

Link to this Internet site from http://www.myreportlinks.com

▶ Today In History
By navigating through this Web site you will find an article discussing
James Garfield's assassination and Chester A. Arthur's succession into
the office of the presidency.

Link to this Internet site from http://www.myreportlinks.com

▶ Vice President Chester A. Arthur
This page from the United States Senate site gives a detailed discussion
of Roscoe Conkling's political machine, Stalwarts and Half-Breeds, and
factors that contributed to Chester A. Arthur's vice presidency.

Link to this Internet site from http://www.myreportlinks.com

▶ The White House Historical Association
At the White House Historical Association Web site you can explore the
rich history of the White House. You can also take a virtual tour
of the White House and learn about the presidents who have lived there.

Link to this Internet site from http://www.myreportlinks.com

Highlights

1829—*Oct. 5:* Chester Alan Arthur is born in North Fairfield, Vermont.

1845—Enrolls in Union College in Schenectady, New York.

1848—Graduates from Union College.

1854—Admitted to the New York State Bar Association.

1859—*Oct. 25:* Marries Ellen Lewis Herndon.

1860—*Dec. 10:* Son, William, is born.

1861–1862—Serves in the New York State Militia during the Civil War, reaching the rank of brigadier general.

1864—*July 25:* Son, Chester Alan is born.

1869—Appointed legal counsel to the New York City tax commission.

1871—Appointed collector of customs of the Port of New York by President Grant.

   —Daughter, Ellen Herndon Arthur, is born.

1878—Suspended from his position as collector of customs by President Hayes.

1880—*Jan. 12:* His wife, Ellen Arthur, dies.

   —*Nov.:* Elected vice president of the United States.

1881—*March 4:* Begins serving as President James A. Garfield's vice president.

1881—*Sept. 20:* Becomes president of the United States when President Garfield dies as the result of an assassination attempt seventy-nine days earlier.

1884—Loses the Republican Party presidential nomination to James G. Blaine. Democratic candidate Grover Cleveland is elected president.

1885—Returns to his New York City home and to his law practice.

1886—*Nov. 18:* Dies at his home in New York City.

Chapter 1 ▶

A Nation on Hold, July 2 to Sept. 19, 1881

Vice President Chester A. Arthur wanted the first weekend of July 1881 to be a restful and relaxing one. He had been vice president under President James A. Garfield less than four months. Recently, Arthur had publicly disagreed with the president over some political appointments. He planned to spend the weekend with his political mentor, Senator Roscoe Conkling of New York.

Charles J. Guiteau Shot President Garfield - Microsoft Internet Explorer

File   Edit   View   Favorites   Tools   Help

Address   http://www.americaslibrary.gov/pages/jb_0702_garshot_1_e.html   Go

Done   Internet

▲ *Charles Guiteau shot President James A. Garfield on July 2, 1881.*

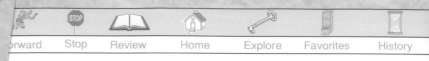

The two New York politicians boarded a steamer in Albany to take them to New York City. During their leisurely cruise down the Hudson River, they discussed political and business matters. When they stepped off the boat, they heard some shocking news.

President Garfield had been shot. His assassin, Charles Guiteau, had been stalking the president for several weeks. Guiteau was mentally unstable. He had supported Garfield for president, and expected to be awarded a diplomatic post. When he was politely but firmly rebuffed, Guiteau decided that Garfield must die. The first reports of the shooting incorrectly said Garfield was dead. Later reports described President Garfield's condition as grave with little hope for recovery. Arthur's response to the assassination attempt was one of grief, shock, and disbelief.

A private carriage quickly took Arthur and Conkling to a hotel. Vice President Arthur was able to avoid reporters for a few hours. After agreeing to see a reporter, he simply said: "What can I say? What is there to be said by me? I am overwhelmed with grief over the awful news."[1]

Arthur spent the next few hours conferring with political colleagues. What should he do? If he stayed in New York, he would look like he was indifferent to the president's pain and suffering. If he rushed off to Washington, it would appear as though he was too eager to take over.

Arthur left for Washington only after learning the president's Cabinet wanted him there. When the president appeared to be recovering, the vice president returned to his home in New York City. He remained secluded from reporters.

By late August, Arthur found himself in the middle of a full-blown constitutional crisis. The Constitution clearly

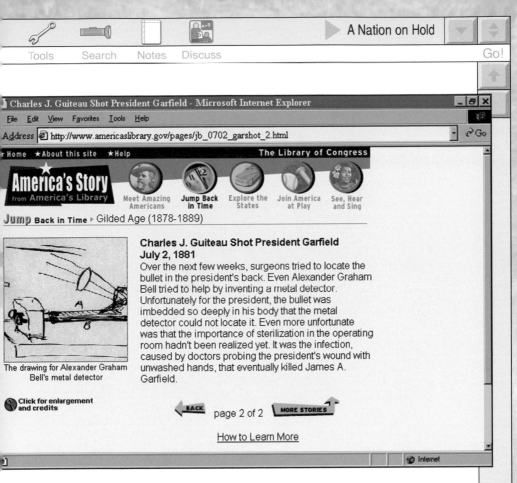

Charles J. Guiteau Shot President Garfield - Microsoft Internet Explorer

File Edit View Favorites Tools Help

Address http://www.americaslibrary.gov/pages/jb_0702_garshot_2.html Go

Home ★About this site ★Help   The Library of Congress

America's Story from America's Library

Meet Amazing Americans | Jump Back in Time | Explore the States | Join America at Play | See, Hear and Sing

Jump Back in Time ▶ Gilded Age (1878-1889)

Charles J. Guiteau Shot President Garfield
July 2, 1881

Over the next few weeks, surgeons tried to locate the bullet in the president's back. Even Alexander Graham Bell tried to help by inventing a metal detector. Unfortunately for the president, the bullet was imbedded so deeply in his body that the metal detector could not locate it. Even more unfortunate was that the importance of sterilization in the operating room hadn't been realized yet. It was the infection, caused by doctors probing the president's wound with unwashed hands, that eventually killed James A. Garfield.

The drawing for Alexander Graham Bell's metal detector

Click for enlargement and credits

BACK   page 2 of 2   MORE STORIES

How to Learn More

Internet

▲ Alexander Graham Bell invented a metal detector in order to locate the bullet embedded in President Garfield's body.

stated that the vice president would take over the duties and powers of the presidency if the president left office because of death, resignation, or removal. Yet no provision was made for the vice president to take over if the president were dying or disabled. No such provision would be added for over eighty years.

Vice President Arthur steadfastly refused to take over. Privately he prayed for President Garfield's recovery. Arthur's close friends worried about his health. The stress, anxiety, and uncertainty he endured took a toll on his physical well being.

The days of waiting and wondering ended on September 19, 1881. Seventy-nine days after being shot, President Garfield died. At 11:30 P.M., a messenger informed Vice President Arthur that Garfield was dead. A pack of reporters hurried to Arthur's house and asked for a statement from the vice president. Arthur's doorkeeper, Alec Powell, refused them entry.

"I daren't ask him," Powell told the reporters, "he is sitting alone in his room sobbing like a child, with his head on his desk and his face buried in his hands. I dare not disturb him."[2]

Early in the morning of September 20, 1881, New York Supreme Court Justice John R. Brady arrived at Arthur's home. He administered the presidential oath of office to Arthur at 2:15 A.M. Chester A. Arthur was now the twenty-first president of the United States.

A grieving nation felt a sense of relief over the transfer of power. Yet many people were concerned about the country's new chief executive. Before becoming vice president, Chester A. Arthur had never held elected office. He was practically unknown outside of New York. Two years before running for vice president, Arthur had been suspended from his job as collector of customs for the Port of New York. Americans wondered how a man who could not run a customs office could lead a nation.

One person who expected Arthur's performance to be excellent was Ohio Governor Charles Foster. He predicted: "The people and politicians will find that Vice President Arthur and President Arthur are different men."[3]

Formative Years, 1829–1856

Chester Alan Arthur was born on October 5, 1829, in Fairfield, Vermont. He was the fifth child and first son born to the Reverend William Arthur and Malvina Stone Arthur. Chester was named for Dr. Chester Abell, the doctor who delivered him.

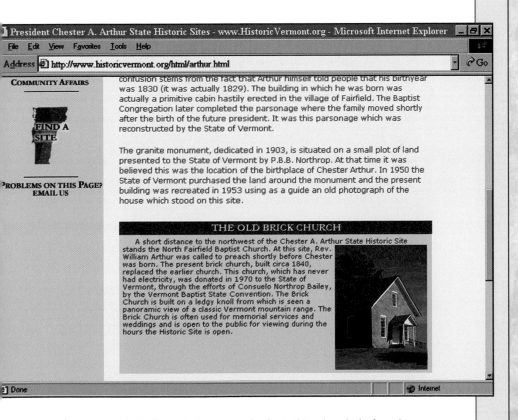

President Chester A. Arthur State Historic Sites - www.HistoricVermont.org - Microsoft Internet Explorer

File   Edit   View   Favorites   Tools   Help

Address http://www.historicvermont.org/html/arthur.html

COMMUNITY AFFAIRS

FIND A SITE

PROBLEMS ON THIS PAGE? EMAIL US

confusion stems from the fact that Arthur himself told people that his birthyear was 1830 (it was actually 1829). The building in which he was born was actually a primitive cabin hastily erected in the village of Fairfield. The Baptist Congregation later completed the parsonage where the family moved shortly after the birth of the future president. It was this parsonage which was reconstructed by the State of Vermont.

The granite monument, dedicated in 1903, is situated on a small plot of land presented to the State of Vermont by P.B.B. Northrop. At that time it was believed this was the location of the birthplace of Chester Arthur. In 1950 the State of Vermont purchased the land around the monument and the present building was recreated in 1953 using as a guide an old photograph of the house which stood on this site.

THE OLD BRICK CHURCH

A short distance to the northwest of the Chester A. Arthur State Historic Site stands the North Fairfield Baptist Church. At this site, Rev. William Arthur was called to preach shortly before Chester was born. The present brick church, built circa 1840, replaced the earlier church. This church, which has never had electricity, was donated in 1970 to the State of Vermont, through the efforts of Consuelo Northrop Bailey, by the Vermont Baptist State Convention. The Brick Church is built on a ledgy knoll from which is seen a panoramic view of a classic Vermont mountain range. The Brick Church is often used for memorial services and weddings and is open to the public for viewing during the hours the Historic Site is open.

Done   Internet

▲ Reverend William Arthur preached at this church before his son Chester was born.

Chester Arthur's Parents

Chester's father, William, was a Baptist minister who often traveled from church to church. In his career, William Arthur served at eleven different churches. He had a fiery temper and was prone to arguing. His blunt and tactless manner often turned people against him.

Chester was not much like his father. He was suave, amiable, and easygoing. He would avoid arguments. He knew how to compromise and made friends easily; his father did not.

His mother, Malvina Stone Arthur, was born in Vermont. She met and married William Arthur when she was living in Quebec, Canada. Like her husband, she was very religious. She and William were greatly disappointed that Chester never formally joined a church.[1]

William and Malvina would eventually have eight children. Estimates indicate that William never made more than $500 a year as a minister. That was not a bad income for that time period, but his was a family of ten. He supplemented his income by teaching school, but that did not pay well either.

Little has been written about Chester Arthur's childhood. In the first nine years of his life, the Arthur family moved five times. Such a rootless childhood made it hard for Chester to form lasting childhood friendships. His father's lack of a steady income caused the family to have to move so often. This may account for Chester's financial ambitions as an adult.

Bright, but Not a Top Student

When he was fifteen, Arthur enrolled at the Lyceum in Schenectady, New York. The Lyceum was a private school that prepared students for college. Teachers there remembered him as being an able, polite, and intelligent student. Arthur worked as an editor on the school paper. He also dabbled in politics by attending a political rally for Whig presidential candidate Henry Clay in 1844.

After studying for one year at the Lyceum, Arthur enrolled at Union College in Schenectady in September 1845. His studies at the Lyceum allowed him to enroll as a sophomore. Arthur studied the classical curriculum. He took courses in ancient history, French, and anatomy, along with numerous math and science classes.

Arthur worked his way through college by teaching during winter vacations. He was in the top third of his class and graduated with honors. Still, he is not remembered for being a diligent student. He was fined several times for skipping chapel services and committing various pranks. He was better known for his social skills than his scholarship.

As a student, Arthur supported ▶ Henry Clay (shown here) for president in 1844.

The Teacher Studies Law

In July 1848, Arthur graduated from Union College. He moved to Schaghticoke, New York, and began teaching school. He had previously taught there during winter breaks from college. He did not stay there long. Teaching only paid fifteen dollars a month, and Arthur believed that an eighteen-year-old college graduate could do better. He decided to become a lawyer.

In 1849, Arthur enrolled at a law school in Ballston Spa, New York. He stayed there for a few months. Then he left, probably because of financial difficulties, and moved into the family home at Hoosick, New York. He returned to teaching and studied law part time. In 1851, William Arthur got his son a job as the principal of a private school that held classes in the basement of William's church.

Years later, Arthur's students would remember him as a stern, but popular teacher. Arthur continued to teach full time and study law part time until 1853. That year, he moved to New York City and became a clerk in a law office headed by E. D. Culver. In 1854, Chester A. Arthur became "Chester A. Arthur, attorney at law."

About a year later, he became a partner in the firm of Culver, Parker, and Arthur. Shortly after Arthur joined the firm, Culver was elected to a city judge position in Brooklyn. His courtroom duties took him from the day-to-day business of the firm. Arthur took on many of Culver's cases and responsibilities.

Although he was only in his late twenties, Arthur could savor many successes—a college education, a partnership in an established law firm, and a bright future as a big city lawyer. Yet, he wanted more, and the next few years would bring him more—romance, marriage, family, and a budding career in politics.

Rising Republican, 1856–1865

Despite being a junior partner, Arthur played a prominent role in two of the firm's most important cases. The first was the Jonathan Lemmon case, in which slaves who were being transported to Texas sought their freedom during their stay in New York City. The second case involved Elizabeth Jennings, a black public-school teacher, who after refusing to get off a streetcar reserved for whites was physically removed by the conductor.

▶ Jonathan Lemmon's Case

Jonathan Lemmon, a slave owner, had traveled from Virginia to New York City. He brought eight of his slaves with him and put them up in a boarding house while they waited to be transported to Texas. New York was a free state (slavery was outlawed), and Lemmon's slaves appealed to a free African-American man named Louis Napoleon to help them.

Napoleon enlisted the help of abolitionists—people who wanted to abolish slavery. The abolitionists hired E. D. Culver to plead their case. He argued that since the slaves were in a free state they should be free. A New York judge agreed and ruled that the eight slaves were now free. The decision was appealed but was upheld by the Supreme Court of New York and the Court of Appeals.

Arthur's dislike for the institution of slavery made him a likely person to be chosen to work on the case. The exact extent of Arthur's involvement in the Lemmon case is not

clear. It is known, however, that his active involvement allowed him to collect one-third of the legal fee.

▶ Elizabeth Jennings's Case

The Elizabeth Jennings case ended New York City's long-time policy of racial segregation on its streetcars. After she refused to leave a streetcar reserved for white passengers, a black public schoolteacher named Elizabeth Jennings was physically ejected from the streetcar by its white conductor. Jennings hired Culver's firm to represent her. Arthur was assigned the case.

Arthur argued that the streetcar company was responsible for the conductor's behavior. He also argued that the streetcar company violated a New York law in ejecting her from the car when she was not being a nuisance or causing a disturbance. The jury agreed and awarded Jennings a $250 settlement.

Although he was enjoying his work and his successes, Arthur was yearning for a woman to share and enrich his life.

▶ Unlikely Marriage

In 1856, Dabney Herndon, Arthur's friend and former roommate, introduced the bachelor attorney to his cousin, Ellen. When they met, Ellen "Nell" Herndon was just nineteen. She was a petite, frail, brown-eyed lady with a pretty smile

◀ *After a short courtship, Chester A. Arthur and Ellen Lewis Herndon were married on October 25, 1859.*

▲ *In the spring of 1856, an abolitionist named John Brown led a raid in which five pro-slavery settlers were killed. This mural, by John Stewart Curry, is called "The Tragic Prelude: John Brown."*

and a lovely singing voice. Arthur was six feet two inches tall with black eyes and wavy brown hair. He was quickly smitten. They were an attractive couple. After a short courtship, they became engaged.

Ellen's background was quite different from Arthur's humble origins. Her family had been prominent in Virginia politics and government since the 1600s. Her father was a captain in the navy, and her mother was a well-known Washington socialite. The Herndons owned slaves, whereas Arthur and his father were known for their abolitionist views.

When visiting Ellen's parents, Arthur would avoid talking about slavery.

Arthur knew Ellen was used to enjoying a well-to-do lifestyle. He wanted to provide for her. He thought he could make his fortune by leaving New York and going west. In 1857, Arthur and Henry Gardiner traveled to the Kansas Territory. Arthur had recently left Culver's law firm to form a partnership with Gardiner. They bought parcels of land in Kansas. They planned to make their fortune by selling the land to incoming settlers.

After arriving in Kansas, Arthur did not like what he saw. Abolitionists and pro-slavery forces were fighting to control the territory. Tensions were at a melting point. Pistols and rifles settled disputes rather than judges and juries. The territory soon became known as "Bleeding Kansas." The constant violence and rampant lawlessness made Arthur and Gardiner fearful and weary.

They only stayed in Kansas for about three or four months. While they were away, Ellen's father tragically died in a storm while he was piloting a steamship. Arthur returned to comfort Ellen and her mother. He helped the Herndons settle the captain's estate, and he assisted the widow in relocating to New York City. Chester Arthur and Ellen Herndon were married at the Calvary Episcopal Church in New York City on October 25, 1859. They shared a home with Ellen's mother. Ellen pursued her musical interests by singing in church and performing at benefit concerts to aid charities. Arthur tended to his law practice and became increasingly active in the recently formed Republican Party. He had also become active in the New York State Militia.

Thurlow Weed was a political ally of Chester Arthur.

The first of the Arthur's three children, William, was born in December 1860. Arthur had little time to spend with his newborn son. The practice of law and his avid interest in politics, which had begun when he was a college student, were taking up most of his time. His political activities and connections helped him rise to a position of power and prominence in the militia.

In 1859, Republican Edwin D. Morgan was reelected to a second term as governor of New York. Thurlow Weed, a political ally of Arthur, was one of Governor Morgan's most important backers. Weed got Arthur appointed to the governor's staff.

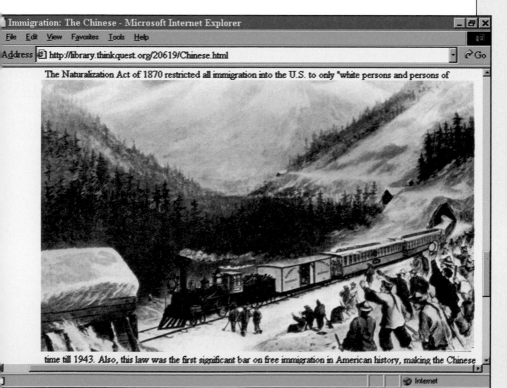

Immigration: The Chinese - Microsoft Internet Explorer

File   Edit   View   Favorites   Tools   Help

Address http://library.thinkquest.org/20619/Chinese.html   Go

The Naturalization Act of 1870 restricted all immigration into the U.S. to only "white persons and persons of

time till 1943. Also, this law was the first significant bar on free immigration in American history, making the Chinese

Internet

Chinese immigrants were hired to work on the Central Pacific Railroad in 1863. The construction of the transcontinental railroad that crossed the Rockies and Sierra Nevada mountain ranges was completed in 1869.

At first, Arthur did not have much to do. In January 1861, he was promoted to the rank of brigadier general in the Union army. His duties were mostly ceremonial, but that abruptly changed with the outbreak of the Civil War in April 1861. Arthur was promoted to acting assistant quartermaster general and stationed in New York City. There he was responsible for seeing that Union troops were housed, fed, equipped, and transported.

Arthur performed his duties with great distinction. Thousands of Union troops passed through New York City en route to their assignments. Arthur worked tirelessly to ensure that they were outfitted for war. In July 1862, he was promoted to quartermaster general with the rank of brigadier general. Along with his other duties, Arthur assumed an increased responsibility for recruiting and enlisting troops.

Governor Morgan praised Arthur's performance when he recalled: "In the position of quartermaster general he displayed not only great executive ability and unbending integrity, but great knowledge of Army Regulations. He can say no (which is important) without giving offense."[1]

Arthur was relieved of his duties after Governor Morgan lost his bid for reelection. He could have re-enlisted, but he opted to return to his law practice. It is believed that his military service put a big strain on his marriage. Ellen and her mother were sympathetic to the Confederacy. Arthur would joke about it by calling Ellen "my little rebel wife," but their opposing loyalties were no laughing matter.

Arthur had no trouble returning to civilian life. The firm of Arthur and Gardiner was soon doing a brisk business. By the war's end, Arthur was ready to cash in on political and economic opportunities. Politics, once his passion, soon would become his profession.

Chapter 4 ▶

Post-Civil War Politics, 1865–1880

By the end of the Civil War, Arthur was firmly aligned with the conservative wing of the New York Republican Party, commonly called the Stalwarts. The Stalwarts steadfastly "held to the Radical Republican shibboleths [catchphrases] of Grant's presidential heyday—the 'bloody shirt,' so-called carpetbag and black rule in the South, hard money, and high tariffs."[1] The "bloody shirt" was the term for how the Republican Party would continue to hold support over an area by saying the South needed to be punished for the bloodshed of the Civil War. Carpetbaggers were Northerners who went to the South to help set up governments and businesses after the Civil War. Arthur's allies, Edwin D. Morgan and Thurlow Weed, were also ardent Stalwarts. Morgan had been elected to the United States Senate in 1863 thanks to political maneuvering by Weed.

In 1867, Arthur was picked to serve on the executive committee of the New York City Republicans. The following year, he became chairman of the party's

Civil War hero Ulysses ▶
S. Grant was elected
president in 1868.

state executive committee. The same year, the Republicans nominated Civil War hero Ulysses S. Grant as their presidential candidate. Arthur served as chairman of the Central Grant Club of New York and worked at fund-raising.

After Grant's election, Arthur hoped to receive an important position in the New York customhouse. Those hopes were dashed when his friend, Morgan, lost his bid for reelection to the U.S. Senate. Still, Arthur was able to get a political appointment.

▶ Boss Tweed and Political Machines

William Marcy Tweed, better known as "Boss" Tweed, was the most powerful Democrat in New York. He created the first big-city political organization. These organizations would come to be called *political machines*. In return for votes, the machine would provide jobs and favors for its supporters. Highly sought after positions went to individuals who had brought in the largest number of votes. In the latter part of the 1860s, Boss Tweed's political machine dominated New York politics.

Tom Murphy, a friend of Arthur, was close to Tweed even though they supported different parties. In 1869, Murphy convinced Tweed to give Arthur a job. Tweed created the office of counsel (attorney) to the New

◀ *William Marcy Tweed, also known as "Boss Tweed," dominated New York's political scene in the 1860s.*

York City Tax Commission. The job paid $10,000 a year and allowed Arthur ample time to continue his law practice.

Arthur did not work there long. He stayed about a year. His exact role and why he left remain a mystery. The Tweed machine was infamous for skimming tax revenues and manipulating tax levies. Arthur was certainly aware of it. Some biographers claim he could not tolerate such rampant corruption. Another explanation suggests that he foresaw Tweed's fall from power and got out at an opportune time.

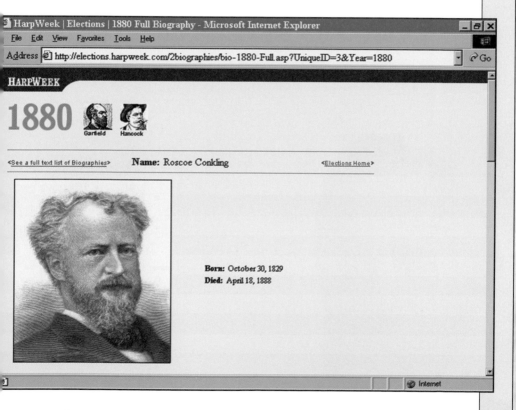

▲ Arthur became an associate of Senator Roscoe Conkling during the late 1860s. Conkling was an ambitious man who wanted to become president himself.

▶ Arthur Finds Conkling to Be a Political Ally

Arthur's strong political connections soon got him another job. His friend, Tom Murphy, had been the collector of the New York customhouse. Unfortunately, Murphy had to resign the position when his close friendship and business deals with Tweed became a political embarrassment. Murphy and New York Senator Roscoe Conkling strongly recommended Arthur as the new collector.

Arthur and Conkling's mutual interest in, and devotion to, politics made them fast friends. Conkling had served as mayor of Utica, New York, before being elected to the House of Representatives and then the U.S. Senate. Conkling was much more ambitious than Arthur. Handsome, highly intelligent, and supremely arrogant, Conkling yearned to become president. Arthur seemed to be more interested in working behind the scenes and living an easy life than attaining political office and power.

▶ Customhouse Collector

President Grant honored their request. In November 1871, Arthur became collector of customs for the Port of New York. He was delighted because the collector's office was a very lucrative position. Under a practice called the "moiety system," the collector was entitled to a portion of fines collected

◀ President Rutherford B. Hayes suspended Arthur from his position as customhouse collector.

by the New York customhouse. Fines were collected when shippers were caught underpaying their tariff. When the moiety system was abolished in 1874, Arthur's income dropped from $56,000 to $12,000 a year.

The moiety system was not the only questionable thing about the New York customhouse. It employed over one thousand workers, and practically all of them were political appointees. Party loyalty and the payment of "voluntary" assessments (financial contributions) to the party were more important than competence and productivity. In 1877, newly elected President Rutherford B. Hayes appointed a commission headed by John Jay to investigate the New York customhouse. Their findings would cost Arthur his job.

When the Jay Commission began their investigation, Arthur was the first witness they called. Arthur spent six hours testifying. He tried to convince the commission that things were being done by the rules, but the commissioners strongly disagreed. The commission found that merit appointments were neglected so party workers could get jobs. They also found that employees were expected to kick back part of their wages to the party.

President Hayes accepted the commission's conclusion that the New York customhouse needed a thorough housecleaning. Rather than fire Arthur, he asked him for his resignation. If Arthur left voluntarily, President Hayes would avoid angering Conkling and the Stalwarts. President Hayes tried to make a deal. If Arthur would resign, President Hayes would make him consul to Paris.

Arthur still refused to resign. President Hayes had no choice. On July 11, 1878, he suspended Arthur and appointed Edwin A. Merritt as the new collector.

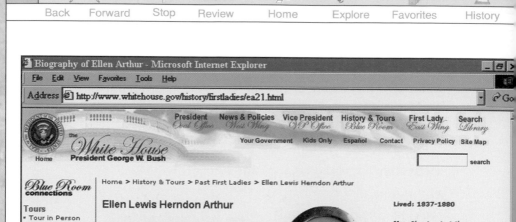

President News & Policies Vice President History & Tours First Lady Search
Oval Office West Wing VP Office Blue Room East Wing Library

Your Government   Kids Only   Español   Contact   Privacy Policy   Site Map

White House
President George W. Bush

Home

Blue Room connections

Tours
• Tour in Person
• Tour On-Line
• Spotty's Tour

Presidents & First Ladies
• Presidents
• First Ladies
• Kids Quiz

White House
• Art
• Blue Room
• Cabinet Room
• East Wing
• Eisenhower Executive Office Building
• Facts
• Oval Office
• Room Descriptions
• Vice President's Office
• West Wing

Home > History & Tours > Past First Ladies > Ellen Lewis Herndon Arthur

Ellen Lewis Herndon Arthur

Chester Alan Arthur's beloved "Nell" died of pneumonia on January 12, 1880. That November, when he was elected Vice President, he was still mourning her bitterly. In his own words: "Honors to me now are not what they once were." His grief was the more poignant because she was only 42 and her death sudden. Just two days earlier she had attended a benefit concert in New York City-- while he was busy with politics in Albany--and she caught cold that night while waiting for her carriage. She was already unconscious when he reached her side.

Her family connections among distinguished Virginians had shaped her life. She was born at Culpeper Court House, only child of Elizabeth Hansbrough and William Lewis Herndon, U.S.N. They moved to Washington, D.C., when he was assigned to help his

Lived: 1837-1880

Mrs. Chester A. Arthur.

http://www.whitehouse.gov/sitemap.html   Internet

▲ Arthur's wife died from pneumonia on January 12, 1880.

Lawyer Turned Political Organizer

Arthur returned to practicing law. His network of friends and political associates gave him enough work to keep him fairly busy. However, law was not much more than a side job. Politics was still Arthur's consuming passion.

In January 1880, Arthur was in Albany helping the Republicans get organized for the upcoming legislative session. A telegram arrived informing him that Ellen was seriously ill. She had caught a cold while waiting outside for a carriage. She later developed pneumonia, so Arthur quickly returned to New York.

He arrived home to find Ellen unconscious after being sedated with morphine. She never awoke. Arthur sat by her bedside for over twenty-four hours before she died on January 12. Ellen Arthur was only forty-two.

Profound Loss, Empty Honors

Arthur loved Nell deeply and he was profoundly grief stricken by her early death. Now he regretted how his absorption and obsession with politics had kept them apart. The late hours and the constant travel had frequently separated them. Late in his life, Arthur would confide to friends that he wished Nell had been there to share his triumphs and honors.

Republican Candidate for Vice President

President Hayes had honored his pledge to serve only one term, so the nomination was up for grabs. Arthur and Conkling attended the convention as delegates pledged to support former President Grant.

In a surprising turn of events, Representative James A. Garfield of Ohio was nominated after thirty-six ballots. To placate the Stalwarts, Garfield offered the position of vice president to one of their own.

James A. Garfield was elected president in 1880. Chester Arthur served as his vice president.

31

HarpWeek | Elections | 1880 Cartoons Navigator - Microsoft Internet Explorer

File Edit View Favorites Tools Help

Address http://elections.harpweek.com/1Cartoons/cartoons-1880f.asp?UniqueID=47&Year=1880   Go

CAMPAIGNING

OVERVIEW

DISCUSSION

"Victory!"

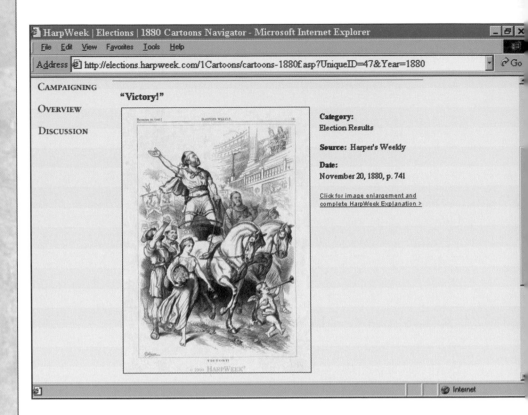

Category:
Election Results

Source: Harper's Weekly

Date:
November 20, 1880, p. 741

Click for image enlargement and
complete HarpWeek Explanation >

Internet

▲ Cartoonist Bernhard Gillam depicted James Garfield as a victorious
Roman general in the November 20, 1880, edition of Harper's Weekly.

His first choice, Representative Levi P. Morton, turned it down. So, the Garfield supporters offered it to Arthur.

Conkling strongly advised Arthur to decline the nomination. Arthur did not follow his advice. He told Conkling: "The office of Vice-President is a greater honor than I ever dreamed of attaining."[2]

Five months later, Chester A. Arthur was elected vice president. Ten months after that, a crazed assassin would make Vice President Arthur the president of the United States.

Chapter 5 ▶

President Arthur, 1881–1885

On September 20, 1881, Chester Arthur was sworn in as America's twenty-first president. The quiet, solemn ceremony took place at his New York City home. President Arthur's first official act was the issuing of a proclamation making September 26 a national day of mourning for President Garfield. On September 22, President Arthur took the oath for a second time. This time the oath

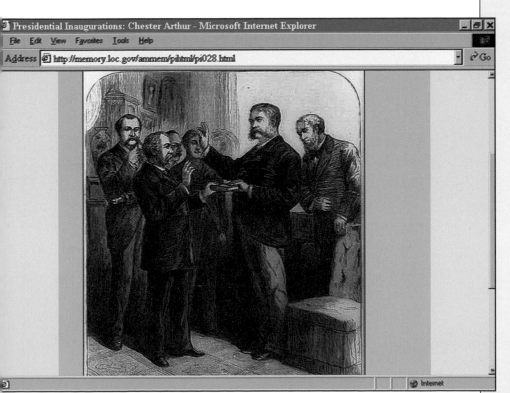

Presidential Inaugurations: Chester Arthur - Microsoft Internet Explorer

File   Edit   View   Favorites   Tools   Help

Address   http://memory.loc.gov/ammem/pihtml/pi028.html

▲ Chester A. Arthur taking the oath of office following Garfield's death.

was administered in the U.S. Capitol Building. Former presidents Grant and Hayes were among the forty or so guests to witness the event.

President Arthur read a brief inaugural address. He stressed the importance of carrying on the work of government by saying: "Men may die, but the fabrics of our free institutions remain unshaken."[1]

▶ Public Opinion Divided

Arthur's restrained conduct while President Garfield was disabled and slowly dying changed public opinion of the new chief executive. Initially, many Americans distrusted him. They wondered and worried how an undistinguished machine politician could effectively lead a nation. There were still doubters and detractors, but now they had to wait and see how he would lead the nation.

On December 5, 1881, President Arthur delivered his first annual message to Congress. He asked Congress to consider reducing taxes, increase the strength and efficiency of the army and navy, and begin providing federal aid for education.

For many years Congress and the federal government had neglected the navy. Many European, and some Latin American countries, had superior fleets. The American ships were mostly made of wood instead of steel, and were powered by sails instead of steam. To correct this, Arthur and Secretary of the Navy William E. Chandler lobbied Congress to authorize increased shipbuilding funds. As a result, funds were approved to build three new armor-plated cruisers and a dispatch boat.

President Arthur also spoke about the need to reform civil service. Since President Garfield's assassination by a crazed office seeker, there was strong public support and

▲ *This political cartoon depicts Lady Liberty mourning the deaths of Abraham Lincoln and James Garfield.*

sympathy for civil service reform. Still, Arthur's support for reform was subdued. He asked for changes to be made gradually. In reality, he secured appointments for many of his friends.

Overall, President Arthur's speech was well received. Many were encouraged by his support for civil service reform. Like all presidents, Arthur would not get everything he asked for. His administration is mainly remembered for new laws regarding immigration, public works projects, civil service reform, and tariffs.

▲ *Thomas Edison was a famous inventor of the Gilded Age.*

▶ The Gilded Age

Arthur became president at a time in United States history that has come to be known as the Gilded Age, or the Golden Age. This period lasted from the end of the Civil War to the early 1900s. It was a time of great industrial growth and invention.

A transcontinental railroad linked the east and west coasts of America, opening the west to further settlement. Inventors such as Thomas Edison (the electric light) and Alexander Graham Bell (the telephone) changed the way Americans lived their daily lives. Business tycoons such as Andrew Carnegie (steel), John D. Rockefeller (oil), J. P. Morgan (banking), and Cornelius Vanderbilt (transportation) amassed huge fortunes.

Still, many people, such as new immigrants that populated the cities, were extremely poor. In addition, there was also a good deal of corruption in both big business and government.

▶ The Chinese Exclusion Act of 1882

Passage of the Chinese Exclusion Act in 1882 marked the first time that President Arthur formally opposed an act of Congress. Starting with the California Gold Rush in 1849, thousands of Chinese had immigrated to America's west coast. Many of them took low-paying jobs building railroads or working in mines. By the 1880s, the demand for cheap Chinese labor waned. The Chinese immigrants were victimized by racial prejudice. There were complaints that they were taking away jobs from white Americans.

Congress responded by passing a bill that banned all Chinese immigration to America for twenty years. President Arthur vetoed the bill, refusing to sign it into law. He favored restricting Chinese immigration, but he felt a twenty-year ban was too extreme. An attempt to override his veto failed. President Arthur ended up signing a compromise measure, reducing the ban to ten years.

The compromise bill still had features President Arthur did not like. It barred United States courts from granting citizenship to Chinese already living in America. However,

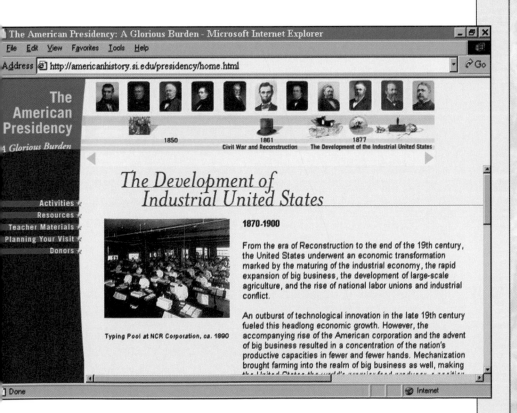

▲ Known as the Gilded Age, the United States experienced rapid industrial growth from the end of the Civil War to the early 1900s.

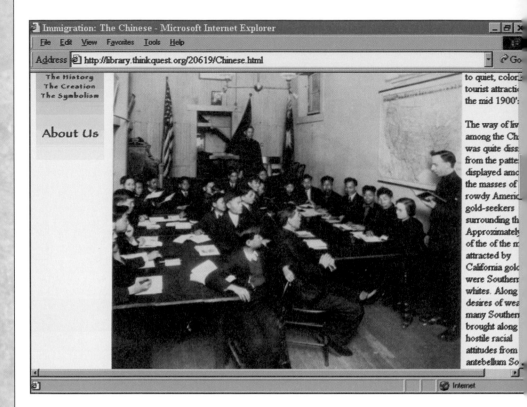

Immigration: The Chinese - Microsoft Internet Explorer

File   Edit   View   Favorites   Tools   Help

Address 🔲 http://library.thinkquest.org/20619/Chinese.html   🔗Go

The History
The Creation
The Symbolism

About Us

to quiet, color
tourist attracti
the mid 1900'

The way of liv
among the Ch
was quite diss
from the patte
displayed amo
the masses of
rowdy Americ
gold-seekers
surrounding th
Approximately
of the of the m
attracted by
California gold
were Southern
whites. Along
desires of wea
many Southern
brought along
hostile racial
attitudes from
antebellum So

🔲 Internet

▲ *In the late nineteenth century, Chinese immigrants took a class to prepare them for naturalization.*

he reluctantly signed it because he knew that if he vetoed the bill Congress would override him and pass it.

▶ Pork Barrel Veto Wins Arthur High Praise

The veto of another bill was headline news across the country. In 1882, Congress voted for an $18 million appropriation in a bill known as the Rivers and Harbors Act. The funds were earmarked for improving roads, harbors, and other public works. Bills like this were known as "pork barrel" bills because they created jobs and government contracts that lawmakers would award to political backers in their state or district.

President Arthur quickly vetoed this bill, but Congress just as quickly overrode his veto. Despite the setback, President Arthur received much praise for opposing what was widely regarded as a raid on the U.S. Treasury.

Tariff Laws Fuel Partisan Differences

In May 1882, President Arthur signed a bill establishing a commission to study and recommend changes in the tariff laws. Since there was a surplus in the treasury, President Arthur had favored reducing tariffs and removing many of the federal excise taxes. The commission issued a lengthy report recommending reducing tariffs by 20 to 25 percent. The commission also favored eliminating tariffs on many imported goods.

Instead of adopting the commission's recommendations, Congress passed its own tariff reduction bill. The commission's findings were largely ignored. The bill passed by Congress only reduced tariffs by 1.47 percent. It was a patchwork law, which became known as the Mongrel Tariff. Many special interest groups would benefit from this bill.

Believing that a bad bill was better than no tariff reduction at all, President Arthur signed the bill into law. In the end, no one was pleased with the law. The passing of the Mongrel Tariff marked the beginning of a long partisan struggle over tariff laws. The Republicans became the party favoring high protective tariffs to make foreign goods more expensive. The Democrats became the party favoring freer trade. Both the Republicans and the Democrats wanted the U.S. citizens to benefit, but they had different views on how this could be accomplished.

Civil Service Commission Established

The most significant law passed during President Arthur's administration was the Pendleton Act. It established the Civil Service Commission and prohibited forced political donations from government workers. This 1883 law also established open competitive exams for job applicants.

The act did not end the spoils system—jobs for valued party members—but it was a vital first step. Initially, it only affected about 10 percent of all federal jobs. Through the years, though, the act was amended and strengthened. President Arthur's strong support of the law surprised his supporters and pleased many of his critics and opponents.

Life at the White House

Arthur transformed the White House into the center of the Washington social scene. Before Arthur, President Hayes had done little entertaining and did not serve liquor at the White House because his wife did not approve of drinking. Under President Garfield, the White House had been a gloomy place because of his assassination and slow death. Arthur had the White House renovated and brought in a French chef to cook gourmet meals. Arthur loved socializing and playing the role of the gracious host. Due to the death of his wife, his sister, Mary, served as the official hostess at White House dinners, parties, and receptions.[2]

Failing Health: Reluctant Candidate

As 1884 approached, it was uncertain if President Arthur would be the Republican presidential nominee. In the 1882 midterm elections, the Democrats gained control of the House of Representatives by securing 62 seats. In the Senate, the Republicans had a slim 38 to 36 majority.

Also, it was unlikely that President Arthur would have the energy and vigor to serve another four years. As early as 1882, he learned that he was suffering from Bright's disease. The disease reduces the filtering ability of the kidneys, hampering the removal of waste products, salt, and water from the bloodstream. In the late nineteenth century, it was a fatal disease. People around the president observed his sluggishness and noted his increasing tendency to put things off.

James G. Blaine, who had served as secretary of state under Presidents Garfield and Arthur, emerged as the favorite to win the Republican nomination. The party was badly split and independent, or "reform," Republican voters still distrusted Arthur. They thought President Arthur was insincere about civil service reform despite his strong support for the Pendleton Act.

▶ Republicans Lose in 1884

President Arthur did not actively campaign to be renominated. When the Republican Party held its national

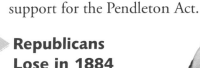

James G. Blaine served as secretary of state under Garfield and Arthur. ▶

convention in June 1884, he did not attend. He stayed at home in Washington. Blaine won the nomination on the fourth ballot. In November, Blaine and the Republicans lost the presidential election to Democrat Grover Cleveland.

During his last six weeks as president, Bright's disease had noticeably affected Arthur's productivity. His close friends became concerned, but the public was unaware of his delicate health. Almost everyday, doctors would quietly enter the White House to treat the president.

Final Years, 1885–1886

President Arthur's final weeks in office were uneventful. He looked forward to being out of the public eye and returning to his law practice in New York City. He anticipated a quiet retirement. When a friend asked about his future plans, Arthur said: "Well, there doesn't seem to be much for an ex-president to do but go into the country and raise big pumpkins."[1]

Arthur was financially secure after the presidency. He owned stock and real estate, and he had been able to save several thousand dollars. Also, Arthur knew he would be earning a good income when he rejoined his old law firm.

▶ Last-Minute Business

President Arthur did not deliver a farewell address. His last major speech was in February 1885 at the dedication of the Washington Monument. Arthur's final act as president was the signing of a bill giving former president and Civil War commander Ulysses S. Grant the full pay and rank of general.

On March 4, 1885, President Arthur and President-elect Grover Cleveland rode in an open carriage from the White House to the Capitol. During the inaugural ceremonies, the outgoing president sat quietly and showed little emotion. After the inauguration, Arthur hosted a luncheon for President Cleveland. In the evening, he attended the inaugural ball.

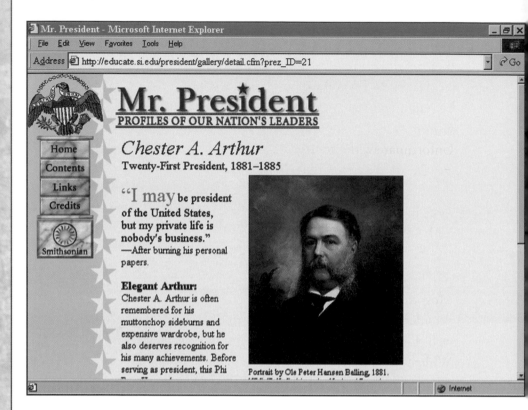

Mr. President - Microsoft Internet Explorer

File   Edit   View   Favorites   Tools   Help

Address http://educate.si.edu/president/gallery/detail.cfm?prez_ID=21   Go

Mr. President
PROFILES OF OUR NATION'S LEADERS

Home
Contents
Links
Credits
Smithsonian

Chester A. Arthur
Twenty-First President, 1881–1885

"**I may** be president of the United States, but my private life is nobody's business."
—After burning his personal papers.

Elegant Arthur:
Chester A. Arthur is often remembered for his muttonchop sideburns and expensive wardrobe, but he also deserves recognition for his many achievements. Before serving as president, this Phi

Portrait by Ole Peter Hansen Balling, 1881.

Due to his problems with Bright's disease, Chester Arthur delivered his last speech in February 1885.

▶ A Dying Arthur Cheers His Friends

Arthur's failing health abruptly ended his plans for an active retirement. He was often too sick to leave his home. Doctors had to make frequent visits to his residence. In February 1886, news of the former president's affliction with Bright's disease was leaked to the press.

By March 1886, finally free from the White House and living in New York City, Arthur knew he was not going to recover. He made out his will. Still, he was able to put on a cheerful and brave front for his friends and loved ones. In a letter to his former postmaster general, Walter

Q. Gersham, Arthur wrote: "My progress in recovering my health is slow and tedious, but I have strong hope that ere (before) this summer is past I shall be good as new."[2]

In mid-November, Arthur surprised his doctors by enjoying a brief recovery. He was able to receive visitors, sign legal documents, and dictate some letters. Unfortunately, the resurgence was fleeting.

On the morning of November 17, 1886, Arthur's nurse found him unconscious. At 5:00 A.M. the next morning, Chester Alan Arthur died quietly at his New York City home.

A Final Assessment

Most historians rank Chester A. Arthur as an average president. Considering his circumstances, he performed well. Elihu Root, who served in the Cabinets of Presidents William McKinley and Theodore Roosevelt, described the difficulties Arthur faced when he became president:

> "He had no people behind him, for Garfield, not he, was the people's choice. He had no party behind him, for the dominant faction of the party hated his name, were enraged by his advancement and distrusted his motives. He had not even his own faction behind him . . . He was alone."[3]

In spite of those obstacles, the Arthur administration reduced the national debt by over $400 million, took steps to modernize an antiquated navy, and reformed the civil service system by passing and enforcing the Pendleton Act. After a tragic assassination, the Arthur administration restored calm and confidence in the federal government.

Overall, Chester A. Arthur's performance as president pleased his friends and surprised his enemies. Many who were skeptics and doubters early on in Arthur's presidency later concluded that Arthur did an able job.

Chapter Notes

Chapter 1. A Nation on Hold, July 2 to Sept. 19, 1881

1. Thomas C. Reeves, *Gentleman Boss: The Life of Chester A. Arthur* (New York: Knopf, 1975), p. 238.

2. Ibid., p. 247.

3. Ibid., p. 245.

Chapter 2. Formative Years, 1829–1856

1. William A. DeGregorio, *The Complete Book of U.S. Presidents* (New York: Dembner Books, 1984), p. 309.

Chapter 3. Rising Republican, 1856–1865

1. Thomas C. Reeves, *Gentleman Boss: The Life of Chester A. Arthur* (New York: Knopf, 1975), p. 30.

Chapter 4. Post-Civil War Politics, 1865–1880

1. Henry F. Graff, ed., "James A. Garfield and Chester A. Arthur," by Bernard A. Weisberger, *The Presidents: A Reference History*, second edition (New York: Charles Scribner's Sons, 1996), p. 274.

2. Thomas C. Reeves, *Gentleman Boss: The Life of Chester A. Arthur* (New York: Knopf, 1975), p. 180.

Chapter 5. President Arthur, 1881–1885

1. Thomas C. Reeves, *Gentleman Boss: The Life of Chester A. Arthur* (New York: Knopf, 1975), p. 248.

2. Paul F. Boller, Jr., *Presidential Anecdotes* (New York: Oxford University Press, 1981), p. 175.

Chapter 6. Final Years, 1885–1886

1. Thomas C. Reeves, *Gentleman Boss: The Life of Chester A. Arthur* (New York: Knopf, 1975), p. 412.

2. Ibid., p. 417.

3. Ibid., p. 419.

Bergen, Lara R., Lisa Hopp, and Angela Tung. *Stuck on the Presidents.* New York: Penguin Putnam for Young Readers, 2001.

Brown, Fern G. and Richard G. Young, ed. *James A. Garfield: Twentieth President of the United States.* Ada, Okla.: Garrett Educational Corporation, 1990.

Clark, Judith F. *America's Gilded Age.* New York: Facts on File, 1992.

Dale, Rodney and Henry Dale. *The Industrial Revolution.* New York: Oxford University Press, Inc., 1994.

DeGregorio, William A. *The Complete Book of U.S. Presidents.* New York: Barricade Books, 1993.

Joseph, Paul. *Chester Arthur.* Edina, Minn.: ABDO Publishing Company, 1999.

Kent, Zachary. *Andrew Carnegie: Steel King and Friend to Libraries.* Berkeley Heights, N.J.: Enslow Publishers, Inc., 1999.

McCormick, Anita Louise. *The Industrial Revolution in American History.* Berkeley Heights, N.J.: Enslow Publishers, Inc., 1998.

Reeves, Thomas. *Gentleman Boss: The Life of Chester A. Arthur.* New York: Knopf, 1991.

Simon, Charnan. *Chester A. Arthur.* Danbury, Conn.: Children's Press, 1989.

Steins, Richard. Hayes, *Garfield, Arthur, & Cleveland.* Vero Beach, Fla.: Rourke Corporation, 1996.

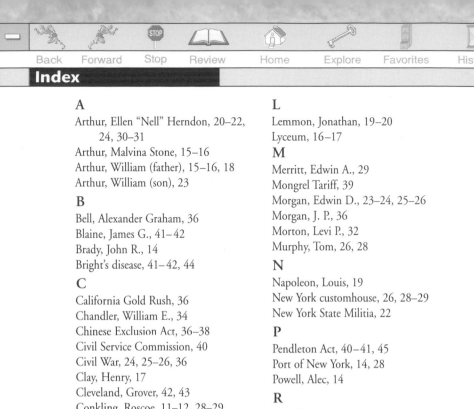

Index